Sunlight and Stones

To you who build with sunlight and stones.

Best wishes,

Thelma Hall

Thelma R. Hall

Shorter College Press
Rome, Georgia

Book design by Marc Bailey of Books International.
Jacket design by Pei-Yen Pan of Emuna Design
Publishing project management by Ross West of
Positive Difference Communications.

Publisher's Cataloguing-in-Publication
(Provided by Quality Books, Inc.)

Hall, Thelma R.
    Sunlight and stones / by Thelma R. Hall.—1st ed.
    p. cm.
    ISBN: 0-9662255-0-3
1. Centering (Psychology)—Poetry. 2. Asia—Poetry.
I. Title
PS3558.A37396S86 1998   8ll'.54
                                      QBI97-41593

First edition: April 1998

Library of Congress Catalog Card Number: 98-60007

For my mother
Lola Mae Mullinax
(1901-1997)
whose strength and simple goodness
inspired me
and
for my husband
Loren Wilson Hall
whose warmth and love
sustain me

Contents

Introduction

Whether reality is gained through experience, imagination, or empathy, the journey of the heart is the same. Sometimes it is not the firm, secure things that bring us the certainty we seek. Often, the small, fragile things guide us by making us careful and aware of our own frailties. Bright moments are tempered by lurking shadows; great joy is tempered by remembrances of pain. The ability to encounter both and rise through pain to find hope is a gift to be treasured. These poems journey through remembrance and imagination, through sunlight and stones, and through their opposites, darkness and fragility, to arrive at a Center Place where their merging brings joy and thanksgiving.

I.

Touching the Familiar

Sunlight and Stones

In a world where sunlight warms
to rich purple fullness
the blackberries hanging almost
within reach
of the small warm hand straining
to win them,

where things are as they seem,
where stones are firm things,
and where toes that clutch
to their rough strong sides
feel in this firmness a sense of security,

How could she have known
that the stone she was standing on
to help fill the distance
from fingertips to berries
would tumble her headlong
into the tangle of briars?

A Revel in Springtime

Ahead of me on the dusty path,
the old barn squats,
fat and heavy, sagging
with its burden.
Bright, glaring colors push
their message into its roof:
"Jesus Saves"

Barefoot, I race past
while warm dust whirls
around my feet.
Spring winds lift my hair.
I could fly with the birds,
dipping, turning and
catching the light, but
the ground is too loving
and pulls at my feet.

Spring Ritual

My father has lain in a grave
for forty years
and the pink lamb marbled above him
wears moss in its ear
from years of dust and rain.
My mother, never one to worship stone,
heeds instead the usurping grass,
wrenching it loose and piling it
roots up to dry in the sun.
It's a losing battle,
the hands aging year by year,
the grass newborn each spring.
But for this one day in May
the hands win, and the grave
blazes with red and yellow roses
and white chrysanthemums, and a few
plastic replicas that alone
will greet the weeds on their return.
My mother is pleased with this ritual
and does not concern herself
with the flat, empty space
beside the double headstone.

Vacancy

Something happens in your heart
when you see no house
where once one stood,
apart from the road, isolated,
but there just the same.

Something fogs in your memory
when you recall fading wallpaper
on a wall no longer there,
and see rickety steps
leading into nowhere.

Something muddles the dream
you have held of carefree childhood
when the places you have played
are too free of familiar boundaries.

Something happens in your soul
when you realize this house
which is no house but vacancy
becomes a prophecy.

Rhythm in Wood

On the top of a hill where oaks still endure
Are remnants that once were a home.
The walls hang loose from the center beams
While the rocks of the chimney stand straight.

Small birds build nests in its rotting boards
And mice multiply in its walls.
My children now sit in its hollow eyes
And dangle their feet down its face.

And when they are told of their grandparents' ways
In the house when the house was whole,
They identify more with the wind in the trees
And the rhythm of their heels hitting wood.

The Merging

Along the path
blackberries hang heavy with dust.
Below, water gurgles and splashes
cool drops upon my feet.
As the sun quivers
over red laurel and gray stones,
I lie down in cool-warm grasses
and remember your touch.
The heavy sun burns
into my flesh
and bird songs wrap about me
as tight as pain.
Then it no longer matters
where the path leads
or who walks there
or why.

River Home

For Wilson

Easy, smooth strokes caress the water.
He is at home with the wind and sun,
with the distant wheeling birds
or those chattering in the tops
of hickories and pines
or the lone blue heron fluttering
on liftoff from still water.

In early morning
he breaks small twigs
and watches fire rise
from the fragile structure.
Smoke hangs in the trees, and
rides on the back of bushes
sprinkled with fog.

Everything is in harmony
except his singing.

On his empty chair,
his warm wrap
curls down to the floor,
waiting.

Rumors of Life

She stood in the doorway
and squinted against the light.
The air beyond the screen
held wavy, tremulous heat.
Silent birds rested in the sultry trees.
Only the steady hum of cicadas
and the hoarse croak of tree frogs
rumored there was life beyond the door.
Then, out of the dense,
oppressive air, she heard
his slow, discordant whistle
shake the lethargic air,
and as she stepped out to meet him,
the startled birds awoke and sang.

Prism

Once, when the sun hid
behind the sugar maple tree
and then shattered into colors
that dotted the brown earth,
I saw you in a different light.
The sun had reddened
in the creases of your eyes
and streaked the hollows
of your cheeks
and muted the harsh complaints
that curved around your mouth.
Sunlight made a prism
of your face.
I longed to know your every turning.

Dream Home

The attic room was full
of flowers.
Chair covers, walls, rugs
glowed yellow and gold.
I rested in the bee-snug cocoon.

Downstairs, the rooms were bare,
and each one teetered
as if sliding down hill.
Closets were tiny and empty of clothes, shoes,
yesterday's keepsakes.
One rambling room's fireplace
gaped cold, prehistoric teeth.

And when I awoke
the dream animal still growled
and the rooms echoed
down long corridors
of restless sleep
until I reached out my hand
and found you
still in the bed beside me.

Hurrying the Harvest

She who was yesterday a child
now turns leaves red
with her touch,
gropes for the roots
of newborn crocus,
tramples down gardens
for the ripened fruit.
She seeks her destination
while I brace against
the pull of the winter wind
and look through its murky curtain
for the signs of spring.

The Passing

"I ran away with your father
in a buggy," she said, reminiscing.
My mind lifted pavement
to see the slow dropping of hooves
and the steady churning of dust.
"I remember Mama turned
from hanging clothes and squinted
against the sun to watch the buggy
out of sight," she said.
This frowning grandmother has no face,
and the woman pressed close against the man
in the buggy is herself half unreal.
"We married in the parlor
of a stranger," she said.
Time blurred the sparse and musty room
and the strange, youthful faces
of these, my parents-to-be.
I rose to go
then felt a keen, sharp pain,
seeing my mother's hand,
and not my own, reach out
from the sleeve of my new coat.

To My Mother, at Ninety-one

Today, I visited the house
where you were born—
at least part of the house.
Present owners wrapped new
around the old, said
the porch floor was made
of the original beams, said
one kitchen wall was a century
old or more.
I tried to claim the wall
with a hand no longer young—
to make it mine, yours, your mother's.
The wood was rough
and unavailing.

Outside, I looked from the porch
where you had hurried away
in a buggy with a man
who would become my father,
where cotton fields had stretched
far into the heat-hazed distant trees.
And for a moment, the fields
became cotton again,
and the mule, sweaty and slow,
moved down the rows
until quivers of heat, distance,
and time blurred the vision.

I looked for you
in bits of plows, harnesses,
tongs, a kraut chopper,
all proudly displayed
on the old-new porch.
But instead, I saw you
as I know you now,
watering your plants,
freezing strawberries, beans,
preparing for tomorrow.

Feeding the Birds

Once, your kitchen sang
and hummed with sizzling skillets,
boiling pots—
chicken browning, corn steaming,
beans bubbling,
and you stirring,
everything cooking on high heat
because you liked the drama
of orchestrated, simultaneous doneness—
lids popping, spoons tap-tapping—
a finale worthy of your watchful conducting.
Leftovers wrapped in tiny bowls
were kept for another meal,
except the bread,
and that you saved to feed the birds.

When your sight was good
and your hearing keen,
you could tell the bluejay from the wren
and the robin from the thrush.
Then, even when you were unable
to see or hear,
you offered them your crusts of bread,
and remembered their music.

Now you lie,
a small, fragile curl of bones,
and no matter how many crumbs
I throw out to entice you,
you will not return to feed.

II.

Like Singing Birds

Conversing in the Street Market

My hands have learned
to speak Chinese—
my student said they flew
like singing birds—
unlike my mouth,
which leaves my Chinese
hanging unattached to meaning
somewhere between
the seller and my needs.
Still, I talk, but the hands
are what the vendor reads.
They gesture, point, measure,
and wave. And while my voice
hangs heavy in the dancing heat,
somehow, as if by miracle,
I walk away with bananas,
ice cream, peanuts, and a smile.
If I was charged too much,
my hands don't know.
By now they're busy speaking
to the passersby and
counting the words
they learned today.

Soft Sleeper Moving to Zhengzhou

The slow train
snakes through China's green hills
that slowly darken into night.
Consciousness of where I am
sings like locusts
through all my waking dreams.
Something is familiar about this place—
something touches the seat
of my first awareness
when freedom raced through all my days.
Small breezes move the curtains
at my feet as I stretch out
in this narrow bed,
and I am lulled to sleep,
rocked by the easy motion
until loudspeakers cut through
the early morning haze
and call this world to work.
They announce my difference,
my alien ways.
I can rise or sleep, sleep or rise,
undaunted by the steely voice
of megaphones in air.

Early Morning in Zhengzhou

I am back in time,
awakening under mosquito netting
in a bed like hard-packed earth.
Faint odors of dust affirm this place.
Long, mournful cries of a steam engine
move through my waking dreams.
Its tremor continues
after the sound fades away.
In the distance a rooster crows.
Outside my window
voices sound strange syllables
my tongue cannot even form.
Silently, gracefully, a man mimes
tai chi exercises,
in touch with something
I can only imagine.
I am a child again—
so much is new, unexpected.
Then gradually, familiar voices
take me back around the world
as I hear American teachers
chatting in the hall.
Familiar and unfamiliar blend
until even in this faraway world
I am at home.

Old Men with Birds

The locusts are so loud
they drive the singing birds to cages.
Then old men hang the cages
on fences and in trees.
The birds sing to them
while they sit and play
at games with wooden pins.
Then, walking home as shadows
darken into night,
the old men talk to the birds
of times when they were young
and watched their fathers
carrying cages in the cold twilight.

Old Woman
at Yantai Church

She stood beside a gray stone wall
like a delicate porcelain vase.
Her small feet touched stone
that ancient slaves
might have carried on their backs
(I wish they could know
that their burden now
is sacred ground).
On her face was a look of peace—
the peace the heart feels
after great pain.

Our eyes met—
our language was a smile.
But what I see now looking back
through the haze and heat
of a Yantai summer day
is a spot of beauty
as enduring as the stones.

Against the Wind

As I rode my bicycle,
hot China wind blew in my face.
Compared with the air
in the sixth-floor room,
this was slightly cooling.
I reflected with pride
that I had pushed to my limit
but still could ride.
I counted the stairs
I had climbed that morning—
twenty-eight flights, back and forth.
But why, I wondered,
did this have to be so hard.
Why must the sun continue to bake my skin
and dry the earth so that dust
flew in my face as I rode.
Then, I met a man almost bent to the ground,
pulling a cart with a heavy load,
his body straining, taut,
his face more tired
than mine has been through all my life.
Then my face burned hot
from shame.

Death in the Model Village Henan Province, China

The Mitsubishi bus empties us
Onto the clean, hard-packed earth streets
of the model village.
We walk through apple orchards,
fields of lotus like great jewels
catching the white-hot sun.
We admire healthy cattle, clean
as though freshly bathed.

Scenes of my childhood
Coalesce—apple trees,
hot sun burning yet
somehow sweet and soothing,
gentle cows munching faraway grass
In another time and place.

We wander down a widening street,
drawn by sounds of oriental music
and by the sight of a small paper house
with blue and yellow streamers
blowing limply in lazy wind.
Here, a dead man lay
waiting for his soul to rise to heaven,
lifted there by the music.
Why can't all death
be a synthesis of rhythm and sun,
jeweled lotus and cows munching grass?

Forest of Stupas

The guidebooks call this place
a forest, a forest of stupas.
Aged stones stand tree-tall
but no birds sing from branches,
no breeze moves the heavy limbs.
Two thousand years ago
the first monk so honored had his bones
enclosed inside this ponderous tree;
then hundreds followed him.

There is a difference between
this forest and a grave.
No names on headstones
speak of death,
and a walk among these stupas
is a warm and friendly visit
with the past,
a merging of stones and trees.

Longmen Caves, Luoyang

Beside the river Yi
the Vairocana Buddha smiles,
immutable against the immensity of time.
Was it wind and rain
that softened this face,
smoothing the harshness of rough stone
or was it gentle hands placating fate,
hoping for grace?
How could those artisans know,
so long ago, that nothing
can appease the angry gods for all time
or hold underfoot forever
the malevolent *yaksha,* no matter
how strong the guard who holds it there.
I reach out my hand to touch
this ancient stone
and wish for some guard against
the evil spirits
that blur my mind
and crumble the idols that I, another
slave of time, have made.

Time and Similes

Small barefoot children
follow me, curious, wide-eyed
as I climb the uneven steps
to the ancient Daoist temple.
I watch them from the corner
of my eye, and when I smile at them,
they turn their eyes away.
I pretend to ignore them;
they step where I have stepped
and huddle close together.
When I turn,
determined to win their trust,
they scurry like frightened geese
and peer at me from behind
the giant gingko tree.

I try to concentrate on the practiced speech
of our guide:
"The ancient gingko tree,"
she says, "looks like a phoenix,
and the mountains in the distance
like a dragon."
But what I see are small faces
who have never seen the likes of me
and are unaware of the weight
of time and similes.

III.

The Miraculous
Commonplace

Nativity in Springtime

For Hannah

A light wind played
about the budded trees—
Laughter and conversation stopped
as family made a warm circle
around the bed
to watch this miraculous
commonplace,
a child born into the world.

There were no sterile halls,
no numbing drugs,
just a fecund house
awaiting the celebration—
and smells of breakfast.

High above, a plane's soft hum
proclaimed a going or a coming home,
and near the window a redbird
sang in full-throated ease.

The early morning light
flowed into this uncommon day
as Hannah greeted a smiling world.

Deception

Houses keep nature out.
The green carpet copies grass
and beams of light hop about
like crippled birds.
Leaf shapes play as shadows through the curtains.
Rain knocks at rooftops, at windows, but
it can't come in.
Sunlight diffuses through windows
seeking pale-leafed plants
that have never felt the wind.
My red-flowered hibiscus smiles at me by day
and dies at night.

Outside, we pick up pieces of nature
and put them in our pockets:
a perfect red maple leaf to brown in a book,
a stone, sparkling with stream water
to dull in a vase.
Fine bright thoughts of things that last forever
mingle with brilliance of leaves
until they, too, fall in wind.

The Plastic Surgeon

He speaks to us of poetry.
Usually, his eyes see
malignancies of form,
and his hands carve between
bones and nerves, making fine
distinctions.
Now, he talks of carving
poems, creating lines,
searching mind banks
for the right word
to place just right
beside another.
No wonder he seeks
the poet's way
between patients.
The poet can erase,
mark through, crinkle
the whole and start over
while the surgeon must live
with the tenuous perfection
his hands have shaped in flesh.

Bystanders

Chickens never seem to know
when they're dead—
the twist and sudden snap
of the neck, the head left
like a grotesque hand puppet
staring glass-eyed from the hand,
the body flopping feathers
over red grass and stones
then twitching, twitching
long after you've turned
your eyes away to glimpse
the last red stain of sunset
spreading its random smear
like a crayon drawing of a child
over the violated yard,
over the crepe myrtle bushes,
over the contented live chickens
pecking crumbs thrown from the kitchen door.

Bird in
The New York Times Building

A bird soars, somewhere,
here, in a mind unfit to tour.
Its wings hold the air
there, turning in sunlight.
The clump of weary feet
beats down on grimy steps
to the bowels of *The New York Times.*
Twenty stories under sky
I hear bird songs
while monotonous presses
stress to a million minds
the irrelevancy of birds.
But above the rattle and roar,
before deafening deadlines
confined reality within walls,
calls of the bird, gliding,
riding the steady current,
spoke to me a fresh green song
that will be news even tomorrow.

Waiting for Breakfast

I finish the second cup of coffee,
remain patient and smile at the waiter,
but still he doesn't stop at my table.
I fold and refold the napkin,
look about me for a familiar face,
find none.
Across the room, looking out
from long blond hair,
a girl in a backless dress
is eating.
Her serene nonchalance makes me fidget,
pull at my clothes, become impatient.
Still no breakfast—
one Casablanca fan,
no Bogarts,
one Lauren, eating.

Trophies of the Surgeon

Animals stare at me
from the surgeon's waiting room wall,
dumb in their intolerable beauty—
all males, past their prime,
the hunter's creed.

I run in the clean mountain air
with the crazed caribou
and share his anguish, betrayed
by his maleness in rutting season.
I run high over perilous slopes
with the Dall sheep.
The hunter must climb to our level
and stalk us with binoculars.
We hide in the snow
but our horns betray us.

I await the comforting words
of this surgeon, whose hands
as skilled as his gun
left me hollow, aged beyond my years.
No portraits of children
will hang upon my wall.

Epiphany

It was an ordinary night
except that he had forgotten the garbage.
Slippered, robed, he began the task.
Cans rattled and neighboring dogs
barked their disapproval.
Cats followed the scent of tuna;
a gush of water hosed down
the offending can.
And then the extraordinary sky
caught him off guard.
There, as clear as if beamed
upon a screen, glorified Andromeda
gleamed above him, loosed from her chains.
He traced her lines
with his naked eyes,
felt the immensity of sky upon sky,
while the small earth's refuse
accumulated unnoticed
around his feet.

The Wolf Is at My Door

The wolf is at my door
but I don't see it.
My pantry is too full
and the starving children
too far away.

I remember hot summer days
and a watermelon's heart
scooped out with my hands—
the rest left to rot in the sun.

Once I ate so much
I was retching sick
and had nightmares
of stick-figured children
with balloon bellies
and bulging eyes.

Today, a large red apple
fell from my too-full sack
and rolled to a gray stone wall.
An old man slowly stooped
to gather the bruised prize into his hand.

Momentous Things

She was not amazed
when water gurgled underground,
sucked down by some
protean mouth,
nor shocked when
bodies or hearts
turned to stone
from looking back.
No molten lava blasting
from an angry earth
distressed her.
These were the things
of myths and gods.
The only things that
chipped away the armor
of her smile
were the eyes of a hungry child,
the hurt on the face of a friend,
a passing thought of loss
that clung to the heavy air
like moss on stone.

IV.

Quiet Despair

The Dancer

For Franziska Boas

This woman who once danced
lithe as a reed in easy wind
now moves dull feet,
hesitates, and forgets the coffee
she holds to warm her hands
in damp, cool April.

Outside, green throbs
through yesterday's brittle twigs.

Does she remember the earth
she dug up with her hands,
the daffodils she brought
from Sandburg's yard?
Does she know she shared them
with me, that again this spring
they danced in winter's dry weeds?

She looks at me over the coffee cup
with wide, innocent eyes,
wondering who I am.
Though time hides ninety years
behind this blue veil, I hope
that somewhere, deep inside,
a young girl dances still.

Flower Under Glass

It's not my disease that frightens me.
It's not the man and the camera
poised in the two-foot space
near the bed in my trailer
that make me want to run and hide,
though the lenses press me down
like a flower under glass.

What frightens me is knowing
that my face, gaunt and smiling,
will look out from a time and space
no longer there and no longer mine.

Behind the Glass

Somewhere, in a picture
she had seen,
a young girl pressed
her broken face
against the windowpane
as neighbors peered back
over their shoulders toward the glass.
Other times she saw this girl
running face to the wind
to hide in snow.
But mostly she saw her
light as air
dancing about the streets,
singing to the birds
and chasing yellow butterflies
that cut clean patterns in blue sky.
She wrote poems about these things
and never hunted snow
and never thought the face
against the window
was her own.

Evicted

I can't keep guard forever
over damask scraps and silver spoons.
I no longer remember the time of their use.
Inside, mice leave black trails,
and roaches flee, frustrated,
from empty rooms.
Stacks of old news
now sog in winter drizzle—
I read my eighty years
in their mottled blur.
I watch as strangers close trunks
over treasures only I had prized,
and listen as motors race away.
Bits of me will rot in strange rooms
farther away than I have ever been.
In nearby houses, neighbors
lie beneath the covers in clean rooms.

Old Man in Water

"I will wash away your sins,"
the preacher said,
"and make you white as snow."
Though my old man's face
betrays me,
for one willed moment
I am a newborn child,
conscious only
of the life-giving water
and the hands that caress
my soft young skin.
But when I emerge,
the sun glares into
my wrinkled soul,
and the water
turns to ashes at my feet.

Street Preacher

Black face shining
through early morning haze,
she paces the corner
and hurls her words
to a neutral sky.
One hand holds her open bible
and the other one shouts
a silent "Repent!"
to passing motorists
hurrying under the light
while the arrow is on green.
Tomorrow she'll preach
to another corner,
but the echo of her warning hand
will still bounce through
the hollows and empty places
where she's been.

Riding Underground

We travel with a mass
of set and unsmiling faces,
each one absorbed in his own
isolation—lost in newspapers,
crossword puzzles.

Musicians play in hollow,
echoing tunnels,
losing their talent
in the hurried, noisy indifference
while above the ground
chamber music and symphonies
exult in shared harmonies.

What leads us on through
the click of cards
in machines, through tunnels
of tiled art, city posters,
through poetry and philosophy
on tube walls
while the eyes around us
stare blank and unavailing,
quietly despairing of
poetry and song?

The Visit

They said that she could sit
like that all day,
her tiny body framed
within the large straight chair,
her eyes unaware of the change
that came into her room
when the opened door
threw our shadows across the floor.
The sunlight from the window
high above her head
fell in a filtered heap
across her lap,
where her thin long fingers
stroked a piece of flannel cloth.
The heavy door closed back again,
but more than the memory
of her smallness in the chair
followed me.

Soldier with Child: 1942

Child of one year
clutched white against my chest
you reach out from me
fearing the long ride
into worlds where white
is forever blasted
and where the place
you long to be
is so far away
even memory is a black wall
touched with red.

That August Morning

"I was upstairs, and then a sudden
Flash came through the window and a
gust of wind blew me on the floor . . .
when I stood up, the roof was gone. . . .
You looked toward the city and the
whole city was burning. . . ."
—Margaret Tanaka

Oh, Hiroshima,
I came to mingle my mother's ashes
with your flowers and sparkling water,
but now they lie with twenty of our kin.

That August morning, I lingered in my room
and did not hurry to the sun and wind.
At fourteen I was shy.
Below, a neighbor talked to grandmother.
He had come to borrow nails.
Standing in the door, he blocked my way.
Outside, the sun and wind waited
and then exploded.
In the distance the city burned.

I wanted to run from the light
but grandmother was old.
We walked, too shocked for fear.
Around us lay blackened shapes
we could not bear to recognize.
I clutched the vase with mother's ashes
to my heart.

No birds sing now in Hiroshima
though peace has settled in ashes and debris.
But always I see the burning,
and blackened faces scream at me
in my sleep.

Scholar Lost Among Boxes

He is in a familiar place
but he cannot find his way.
Around him stare blank-faced boxes
A-C, D-F. . . .
Inside the boxes,
thousands of smaller files
sort, alphabetize, arrange
by type: Nouns, Verbs,
Adjectives, Adverbs.
He consults for dictionaries,
encyclopedias, is expert
in roots, origins, meanings.
But today, his fingers move
frantically through one file
after another, searching
for the origin, the meaning,
the name for the hollowness
that echoes through him.
His fingers search,
night falls slowly,
and he is unaware
when the morning comes.

The Locksmith

He walks or sits
folded inside himself,
a self-seal envelope
marked return to sender.
The tiny shop smells of metal,
a scent his hands will carry
to his grave.
He is a deadbolt lock
without a key.
In his dreams he hears tumblers
trying to align,
sees wings sprouting
from his ingrown shoulders,
feels ideas spreading bright
as peacock feathers
from his opened mind.
But always, he awakes
before the key is turned.

Child from the Water

Her body glistened
as she bathed among the rushes,
handmaidens shielding her.
Lithe as the reeds around her,
she longed to swell and bloom
and bring forth a child of her own.
She cupped her hand
and drew the water to her body.
Small drops trickled back
to the ancient stream.
Then the reeds in front of her parted,
nudged by a bobbing basket.
She thought of stories told of infants
set afloat to drift the Nile
or left to die upon the mountains
and be the meal of dogs,
of mothers weeping
and of her own silent aching.
She motioned, and the tiny ark
was brought up to her.
She lifted the baby from the water
and held him close.
His tiny hand was a fist
Upon her breast.

The Chosen

Japheth dragged his feet up the gangplank
where safety was raucous sounds of animals.
He fought against the force that pulled him back.
For weeks he had strained his heart
toward heaven for answers.
He could read the hurt
in his father's grizzled face and brow
and knew that except for him
he would have been struck dead
for daring to question.

But Japheth loved his neighbor's small son
who often sat upon his lap and laughed
like one who had happiness for his drink
instead of the bitter draught his parents
poured into his cup.
And he loved the wizened old one down the road
whose curses sent chills riding down
the backs of the righteous.

Love plucked Japheth's heart and left it barren,
and neither the comforting swish
of his wife's rough skirt
ahead of him on the ramp
nor the knowledge that he was chosen of God
could save him.
Wherever his feet touched
when the earth appeared again,
he would step on those whose love
still screamed into his dreams
and cracked and crumbled each new wall
he built to shield him from the hurt.

V.

Reaches Through Pain

Where Beauty Lies

Brilliant shards of glass,
edged with blood,
glint in the sun.

Gaunt-eyed villagers
huddle in ruins
surrounded by green grass
and yellow flowers
jubilant with springtime.

The human heart
is also a paradox,
exulting in beauty
amid atrocities of pain.
Sometimes it must
reach down deep
for the bright shard
untouched by red.

A Rustling in the Wind

Sometimes it's just a vague uneasiness,
leaves rustling before they fall.
Someone stops to tie a shoe
and unconsciously you view
a broken string, a staring child.
You feel a hurt for something, somewhere.
A man stands blind on the corner,
and you wish you were blind to him.
A woman walks by without a coat,
and a cold wind creeps into your heart.
Someone speaks to you of trouble
and a heavy anxiety hangs over
your child. What if? Suppose?
Sometimes you wonder which is worse,
the rustling or the fall.

The Winner

I hold in my hand
the tooth of the tiger—
a bantering of minds
regressed to brute force
and a brandishing of wills
until superior strength
declared me winner.
I don't recall the gaff and gouge,
the twist and pull of excising,
only the beauty and power
of the final surge
and glaring teeth
that tore from me my vital parts
but left the trophied hand.

The Victim

Long before the legions of memory
marched with flashing arrogance
into the heart,
a sly, insidious scout sneaked,
stealthy as a cat upon a bird,
past the carelessly guarded
fortress of the brain,
and planted his cocklebur
like dynamite, retreated
suddenly, imperceptibly,
as twilight into dark,
waited for the long fuse
to reach its target
explode
and leave its victim
helpless
for the slaughter.

Battling the Elements

You can sandbag the door,
nail crossing bars over windows,
prop up the roof with steel
and anchor the floor in cement,
but just as you settle
into acceptance of creaks
and thumps and moaning wind,
under the doorway will creep
the subtlest of memories
to startle and shake the peace.
It comes in the night
in the shape of dreams,
in the middle of sun-bright thoughts
of hope and love.
Sometimes, determined to invade,
it rattles the protective bars,
floods and threatens to drown,
then coats the survivor
with mud and debris.
It bends and breaks,
or warps at the least,
all foundations.

What is it that says
"Build again, this time
on higher ground
or snug under a mountain's shadow,"
and makes us listen and begin anew?

Going Home

Four-lane roads split billboards and trees;
tall nodding grasses beard balding slopes.
Two-lane roads curve past houses with porches,
Rock City barns and Get Right With God yards.
One-lane roads send dust clouds flying
over sagging houses; nearsighted hens
squint in the yards.
Sweat runs down into
landscapes of flesh.
Deep-rutted paths
tangled in vines
narrow memory.
No one is home here,
but behind,
the road is obscured
and I cannot return.

Betrayal

The sun freezes the upturned roots
of the largest oak tree in the yard.
Its limbs once swept down
upon the roof and sent leaves
reeling bright as hope
over the browning yard.

The moon is a black snarl
in an orange sky.

Outside my window
birds sit dull-eyed and silent.

Your eyes on me see bone, not flesh,
and my eyes looking back
are the owl's, the dove's,
the mockingbird's.

In the valley an eagle circles,
looking for its mate.

A Mourning in Spring

Blue sky muted the harshness
of heavy wood, and bright sunlight
etched warm patterns
on flesh, wood, and earth.
Red drops gathered
to the right, to the left,
and in between.
Both rabble and beloved
watched and waited.
Near the edge of the crowd
a young boy buried his face
in his hands and prayed
for roses to rise
out of the red stain
and for peace to settle
like a blue fog
over the violated land.

Traveling to Brno

The road winds
upward,
a small gray line
through flowering
apple trees.
In the distance,
red roofs dot
the green world
we ride away from
and into.

Counterpoint

St. Charles Cathedral
startles my senses,
diminishes me, fragile
beside its massive,
delicate grandeur.

Inside,
statues of Jesus hang
stark white
against heavy, ornate wood.

The dust rises
around your feet—
your simple robe
drapes loosely
around your body.

Crowds walk in awed silence
or snap photographs
in vain attempts to capture
the beauty and meaning
of stained windows.

Sun beams down
and your hair hangs
damp upon your shoulders
as you disappear
into the waiting crowd.

As I drag my feet
along the cathedral floor
in a beam of spangled light,
I wish for the smell of dust,
the heat of passion, the will
to suffer, the grace
to slip away
and walk the simple path.

Auschwitz, 1996

for Alina
who survived

Within the walls of Auschwitz
I met you, my sisters.
Your pictures line the walls
of my heart.

As I hold the iron railings
that shut you from the light,
I feel my body being pulled
 into your cell.

I stand stripped bare.
Only clothes, shoes, hair
speak of my outer being.
I assert my soul's pride.
It needs no outer cover.

I stand, one body with many,
waiting for the cleansing shower
but drown instead
in my lungs' blood.

My flesh becomes bone,
then ash, sprinkling
the countryside.

. . . .

My mind calls back my flesh:
When I breathe again,
I am no longer ash
falling like black snow.
I float over the fence
where yellow flowers
embrace me, saying
"Come, the soul is
no longer blackened
with pain."

My heart constricts
but will not harden—
someday, it will
sing again.

Oh Helena, Magda, Maria,
look up—
Alina's bird hovers overhead.
We will live again.

To Wake Up Singing

What does it take
for us to wake up singing,
feeling joy rise
from the Center Place?

Through a clamoring
in the wind
and a hammering
in the rain,
we have to listen
to our hearts
though they speak as softly
as the falling snow.

To wake up singing
we have to feel hope rise
so warm we want to touch it
and hold it in our hands.

Though the sunlight flirts
with the beckoning dark,
we have to bend our wills
to the voice inside
pushed by the force
that asserts "I am."

To wake up singing
we have to feel God's grace
touch our souls
like a cooling mist,
see His love
in the rain and dark,
find our voices
through the rumbling thunder,
then sing our songs
from the Center Place.

Acknowledgments of Previous Publication

Previous publication of the following poems is acknowledged:

"Auschwitz, 1996," in archives of the United States Holocaust Memorial Museum, Washington, D.C.

"Betrayal," *The Chattahoochee Review.*

"Bird in *The New York Times* Building," *The Scribbler; The Chimes.*

"Bystanders," *The Reach of Song,* Yearbook of the Georgia Poetry Society, Book 5.

"Child from the Water," *New Poet's Review.*

"The Chosen," *The Reach of Song,* Yearbook of the Georgia Poetry Society, Book 2.

"Death in the Model Village, Henan Province, China," *Number One,* Vol. 15.

"Deception," *The Chimes; Number One,* Vol. 18.

"Dream Home," *Number One,* Vol. 21.

"Epiphany," *The Reach of Song,* Yearbook of the Georgia Poetry Society, 1989-90.

"Evicted," *The Old Red Kimono.*

"Flower Under Glass," *Number One,* Vol. 12.

"Going Home," *The Reach of Song,* Yearbook of the Georgia Poetry Society, 1989-90.

"Hurrying the Harvest," *Number One,* Vol. 14.

"The Locksmith," *Perceptions; The Reach of Song,* Yearbook of the Georgia Poetry Society, Book 6.

"The Merging," *Georgia Journal.*

"Momentous Things," *American Poetry Anthology.*

"A Mourning in Spring," *Georgia Journal.*

"Nativity in Springtime," *Cotton Boll/Atlanta Review.*

"The Passing," *The Reach of Song,* Yearbook of the Georgia Poetry Society, Book 5.

"The Plastic Surgeon," *Number One,* Vol. 23.

"A Revel in Springtime," *The Reach of Song,* Yearbook of the Georgia Poetry Society, Book 4.

"Riding Underground," *Number One,* Vol. 21.

"A Rustling in the Wind," SCETC *Newsletter.*

"Soldier with Child: 1942," *The Chimes; Number One,* Vol. 16.

"Spring Ritual," *Poem,* No. 39; *The Reach of Song,* Book 3.

"Sunlight and Stones," *The New Laurel Review.*

"Trophies of the Surgeon," *Southeastern Miscellany.*

"Vacancy," *Georgia Life.*

"The Victim," *The Dekalb Literary Arts Journal.*

"The Visit," *Number One,* Vol. 19.

"Waiting for Breakfast," *The Habersham Review.*

"The Winner," *Poem,* No. 35.

Poems about China from Chapbook, *Among Chinese.*